W9-BPP-479

DISCARDED

2013 Back to Books Grant

Purchased with funding provided by

The Illinois State Library &

The U.S. Institute of Museum and

Library Services

# Forces and Motion in the Real World

by Kathleen M. Muldoon

**Content Consultant**
J. M. Collins, PhD
Associate Professor of Physics
Marquette University, Milwaukee, Wisconsin

CORE
LIBRARY

Published by ABDO Publishing Company, PO Box 398166, Minneapolis, MN 55439. Copyright © 2013 by Abdo Consulting Group, Inc. International copyrights reserved in all countries. No part of this book may be reproduced in any form without written permission from the publisher. The Core Library™ is a trademark and logo of ABDO Publishing Company.

Printed in the United States of America,
North Mankato, Minnesota
112012
012013

♻ THIS BOOK CONTAINS AT LEAST 10% RECYCLED MATERIALS.

Editor: Karen Latchana Kenney
Series Designer: Becky Daum

Cataloging-in-Publication Data
Muldoon, Kathleen M.
 Forces and motion in the real world / Kathleen M. Muldoon.
   p. cm. -- (Science in the real world)
Includes bibliographical references and index.
ISBN 978-1-61783-740-1
1. Force and energy--Juvenile literature.   I. Title.
531--dc21
                                        2012946819

Photo Credits: Emilia Ungur/Shutterstock Images, cover, 1; Jamie McDonald/Getty Images, 4; Stock Montage/Getty Images, 8; Prisma/ UIG/Getty Images, 10; General Photographic Agency/Getty Images, 12; Justin Sullivan/Getty Images, 14; Lars Baron/Bongarts/Getty Images, 16; Encyclopaedia Britannica/UIG/Getty Images, 18; Shutterstock Images, 20, 26; Chris Rutter/N-Photo Magazine/Getty Images, 23; Oleksii Sagitov/ Shutterstock Images, 24; Stephen Mcsweeny/Shutterstock Images, 28; Red Line Editorial, 29, 40; Tom Wang/Shutterstock, 31, 45; NASA/Getty Images, 33; Shaun Botterill/Getty Images, 34; iStockphoto, 37, 38

# CONTENTS

# CHAPTER ONE

# Push, Pull, and Move

When you kick a ball on a field, you know it will move forward. On your skateboard, you know going down a hill will make you speed up. And while gazing at the stars and moon, you are certain they will not suddenly fall from the sky. You know all these things are true. But you might not know *why* they are true.

Forces and motion are at work as a skateboarder gets air during a trick.

## The Hubble Space Telescope

On April 24, 1990, the space shuttle *Discovery* launched a giant telescope into space. The Hubble space telescope is as big as a school bus. It is powered by light from the sun and is controlled by computers. Forces and motion keep the Hubble space telescope in orbit. It sends images to Earth that increase our knowledge of the universe. One image sent in 2011 showed a fifth moon orbiting Pluto.

Physics helps explain what we know or would like to know about how the world and universe works. Scientists have discovered natural laws that rule everything on our planet and the solar system. Some of these natural laws are about forces and motion. Forces are pushes or pulls that can make objects move or stop moving and can change the shape of an object. Motion is any movement or change in position. Without forces and motion, the world could not exist as we know it.

While holding a book, you may think you are sitting perfectly still. But there is motion within and around you. Invisible forces are at work keeping you alive. Your heart pumps blood to every cell in your body. Gravity pulls you toward Earth's center. Outside, birds fly, motors hum, and the whole world is in motion.

## FURTHER EVIDENCE

Chapter One contains quite a bit of information about the study of forces and motion. It covers important scientists who have studied forces and motion. But if you could pick out the main point of the chapter, what would it be? What evidence was given to support that point? Visit the Web site below to learn more about forces and motion in everyday life. Choose a quote from the Web site that relates to this chapter. Does this quote support the author's main point? Does it make a new point? Write a few sentences explaining how the quote you found relates to this chapter.

**Idaho Public Television: Gravity Facts**
www.idahoptv.org/dialogue4kids/season12/gravity/facts.cfm

# CHAPTER TWO

# Studying Forces and Motion

Scientists have been studying forces and motion for centuries. Aristotle was an ancient Greek philosopher and scientist who lived from 384 to 322 BCE. He noticed that four elements made up the world: solids, liquids, gas, and fire. He believed that forces and motion happened when these elements tried to find their place in the world. Scientists later

Philosopher and scientist Aristotle, left, taught his studies to others, such as Alexander the Great, right.

Galileo Galilei studied the stars and thought about the forces on Earth and in space.

used some of his observations to understand forces and motion.

In 250 BCE Greek scientist Archimedes discovered the reason why some objects float and others sink. It depended on the volume of the object and the force of air or water on it. This theory proved to be true. Today engineers rely on Archimedes's discovery. It helps them design ships that float in water and planes that soar in air.

## Modern Physics

Galileo Galilei has been called the father of modern physics. In 1609 CE he developed a telescope. Later in his career, Galileo tried to show that force and motion work together. In one experiment he dropped balls of different

### A New Idea of Motion

Galileo learned about Aristotle's teachings on motion while in college at the University of Pisa. He did not agree with them though. His experiment dropping balls proved that Aristotle was wrong. Aristotle believed the heavier ball should have hit the ground first.

Albert Einstein studied gravity and forces.

weights from a tower. The balls hit the ground at the same time. This showed that objects fall at the same rate even if they are of different weights.

Sir Isaac Newton also discovered laws that run our universe. He added to work that Galileo had done. In 1687 Newton used math to create laws of motion. Scientists still use those laws today. Trains, cars, and spacecraft are designed based on Newton's laws of motion.

Albert Einstein was always interested in laws of nature. In 1907 he released his studies on the laws of gravity. This is the force that pulls you down to Earth.

Perhaps one of the most well-known physicists is Stephen Hawking. He has

## Black Holes

The force of gravity causes black holes. Gravity's force is very strong in certain spots in outer space. A dying star can cause this strong force. It pulls so much that light cannot escape. You cannot see a black hole. But you can see the stars around one.

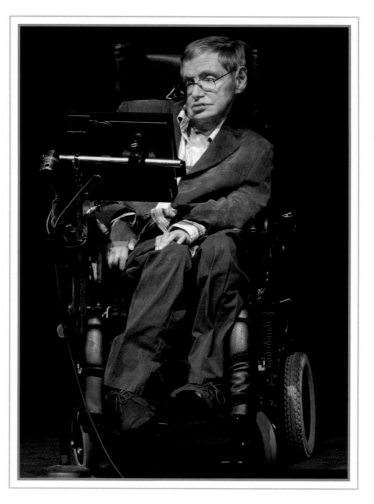

Physicist Stephen Hawking speaks about physics at the University of California, Berkeley, in 2007.

combined some of his theories with Einstein's. One of the many things he studies is how forces create black holes in space. His book *A Brief History of Time* was published on September 1, 1998. It helps us understand the effects of forces and motion in the universe.

In 1752 William Stukeley wrote a book about his friend Sir Isaac Newton's life. In it Stukeley wrote of a conversation he had with Newton:

> *After dinner, the weather being warm, we went into the garden and drank tea, under the shade of some apple trees . . . when formerly the notion of [gravity] came into his mind. "Why should that apple always [fall straight down] to the ground," thought he to himself, occasion'd by the fall of an apple, as he sat in a [thoughtful] mood. "Why should it not go sideways or upwards, but constantly to the earth's centre?"*
>
> Source: William Stukeley. "Memoirs of Sir Isaac Newton's life." Turning the Pages. *The Royal Society, n.d. Web. Accessed November 6, 2012.*

## Consider Your Audience

Read Newton's quote from the passage above closely. How could you adapt Newton's words for a modern audience, such as your neighbors or your classmates? Write a blog post discussing the same observations and questions to the new audience. What is the most effective way to get your point across to this audience? How is language you use for the new audience different from Newton's quote? Why?

# CHAPTER THREE

# Forces Rule!

**F**orces rule our universe, our world, and us. We cannot actually see most forces, but we can feel their pushes and pulls.

There are four main types of forces: strong, electromagnetic, weak, and gravitational. Forces relate to atoms. An atom is the smallest part of all matter. It contains a nucleus made of protons

Wind is a force that cannot be seen, but its effects can be observed.

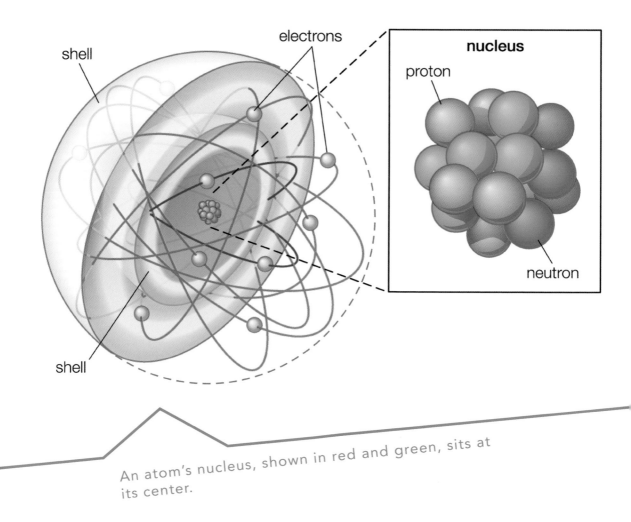

shell

electrons

nucleus

proton

neutron

shell

An atom's nucleus, shown in red and green, sits at its center.

and neutrons. Electrons float in shells around an atom's nucleus.

## Strong and Weak Forces

The strong force is the force that keeps the nucleus together. It is very strong inside the nucleus, but cannot be felt far away from the nucleus. The weak force is the force that causes decay of small particles. Decay is when an atom's nucleus emits particles.

## Electromagnetic Force

Electromagnetic force is seen in the electrical charge in parts of atoms. Electrons have a negative charge. Protons have a positive charge. Protons are attracted to electrons. This holds an atom's nucleus to its orbiting electrons. This force can be felt over long distances.

Friction is an electromagnetic force. Have you walked on carpet and then touched metal? The shock you received is caused by static electricity.

## Magnetic Resonance Imaging

When doctors search for the cause of a person's illness, they may use magnetic resonance imaging (MRI). MRI machines are giant magnetic tubes. The patient slides into the machine on a flat table. After the machine is turned on, it creates a magnetic field. Atoms inside the patient reflect radio signals back to the MRI machine. A computer changes these signals into images of the patient's body.

Gravity holds the moon in Earth's orbit.

As you walk, your shoes rub on the carpet. This causes friction. The friction lifts electrons away from the carpet. Your body is now supercharged! If you touch metal and are in a dark room, you might see a tiny electrical spark jump from your fingers to the metal. This is static electricity, an electromagnetic force.

# Gravitational Force

Gravity is an attracting force between two objects anywhere in the universe. On Earth gravity pulls everything toward its center. Gravity holds the moon, you, and everything else on Earth in place. You can't feel gravity, but it is always working upon you. Because our planet has more mass than the moon, Earth's gravity is stronger than gravity on the moon. Jupiter's gravity keeps at least 61 moons orbiting around it. Not even Galileo or Newton understood the exact cause of gravity's pulling force. But without it, everything in the universe would swirl about and smash into each other.

# The Nature of Forces

Forces rarely work alone. Several forces may act on an object at the same time. For example, Earth's gravity holds ocean water to its surface, but gravity from the sun and moon pull oceans toward them. These different forces result in tides that change the position of the water.

## Using Gravity to Map Mass

On March 17, 2002, NASA and the German Aerospace Center launched two satellites that use gravity to discover changes in Earth's mass. They are called the Gravity Recovery and Climate Experiment (GRACE) satellites. The information these satellites collect helps scientists find out the rate at which polar ice melts. Scientists find out the rate that polar ice melts in order to measure the changes in Earth's temperature. This information is especially useful for understanding global warming.

## Balanced and Unbalanced

Forces don't always make objects move. Suppose a heavy book is placed on a table. The book's weight pushes it down on the table. The surface of the table pushes back on the book with equal force. Since the forces of the book's weight and the surface of the table are equal, they are in balance.

Balanced forces are two or more forces acting on an object at the same time. They do not change an object's motion because the forces are equal in strength.

Ocean tides are pulled and pushed by the gravity of Earth, the sun, and the moon.

Construction cranes use balanced forces to lift heavy objects.

Unbalanced forces are forces that cause a change in an object's position or motion. This is because one force is greater than another.

Stephen Hawking wrote about gravity in his book *A Briefer History of Time*. He said:

> *Gravity is the weakest of the four forces by a long way; it is so weak that we would not notice it at all were it not for two special properties that it has: it can act over long distances, and it is always attractive. This means that the very weak gravitational forces between the individual particles in two large bodies, such as the earth and the sun, can add up to produce a [very big] force.*

> Source: Stephen Hawking and Leonard Mlodinow. *A Briefer History of Time*. New York: Bantam, 2005. Print. 120.

## What's the Big Idea?

Take a close look at Hawking's words. What is his main idea? What evidence is used to support his point? Come up with a few sentences showing how Hawking uses two or three pieces of evidence to support his main point.

# CHAPTER FOUR

# Laws of Motion

**M**otion is about moving. Force gets objects moving. But motion is also about *how* things continue to move after that first force. Sir Isaac Newton discovered three laws that help us understand motion.

## The First Law of Motion

This law has two parts. First an object at rest will stay at rest until an unbalanced force is put on it. For

The force of a push starts the motion of a swing.

A baseball changes direction when it is hit by a batter's bat.

example, if you toss your dirty socks on the bed, they will remain there until you push them off. Second, an object in motion will move in a straight line at a constant speed until an unbalanced force acts on it. When a batter hits a line drive, the ball continues

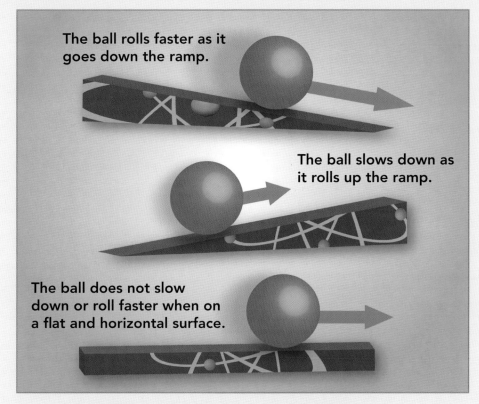

The ball rolls faster as it goes down the ramp.

The ball slows down as it rolls up the ramp.

The ball does not slow down or roll faster when on a flat and horizontal surface.

**Newton's Laws in Action**
This diagram shows how Newton's three laws of motion work upon a ball. The force pushed against the ball is a person's finger. After reading about Newton's laws, what does this diagram tell you? Does it help you better understand how the laws work?

moving forward until it is caught, hits a wall, or meets a force that changes its motion. Objects at rest or in motion in the same direction and at the same speed are in the state of inertia.

# The Second Law of Motion

Acceleration is any increase in speed or change in direction caused by unbalanced forces. When force pushes on an object, it makes the object move in a certain direction. If the force acts in the direction of motion it will make the object have a greater speed. If the force acts opposite to the direction of motion it will make the object have a slower speed. A stronger force will change the motion faster than a weaker force.

## The Motion of Earth's Plates

Massive sheets of solid rock, called plates, are always moving very slowly below Earth's surface. Earthquakes happen when one plate slips past or under another. Scientists use computers to follow the movement of Earth's plates. They combine that information with a measurement of the force of the surface above the plates. This force pushes against the plates. Knowing the force and movement allows scientists to better predict where earthquakes might occur.

# The Third Law of Motion

This law tells us that for every action, there

Wind pushes back as a car speeds forward.

is an equal and opposite reaction. You can feel this law when you ride in a car. As it speeds forward, air pushes back against the car. The car's forward action is a push into the air, which causes the reaction of wind pushing back at the car.

## Motion in Action

Motion affects our everyday lives and our universe. Whether we travel on foot, on a bike, in a car, or through the air, we like to know how fast we will get from here to there. The motion of objects moving in a line is an object's velocity.

Suppose, though, that rather than moving in a straight line, you are a figure skater spinning on a spot in the center of the ice. You are thinking more about staying upright than you are thinking about your speed. Centripetal force causes some objects to move in circles. A satellite orbits Earth because gravity pulls the satellite toward Earth's center.

A research satellite orbits Earth in 1991.

# CHAPTER FIVE

# Motion and Energy

In 1807 English scientist Thomas Young was the first person to study how objects in motion can be made to do work. He believed that the ability of an object to do work was its energy. Forces and motion play an important role in an object's energy. Scientists have found many types of energy. Two major types are kinetic energy and potential energy.

The force of a foot on a soccer ball is changed into the kinetic energy of the ball.

# Kinetic and Potential Energy

Any moving object able to do work has kinetic energy. This is the energy of motion. Moving objects can change from one form of energy to another. For example, whirling blades on windmills convert the wind's kinetic energy into electric energy.

Scientists have also discovered that energy can be stored for later use. Potential energy is one example of stored energy. It is due to an object's position. Imagine an enormous wrecking ball dangling from a cable on a crane. The raised ball has potential energy. Then the crane operator puts the cable in motion and swings the ball into the wall of a building. It crashes through a wall, pushing it inside the

## Kinetic Energy and Sports

Because kinetic energy is the energy of motion, many sports involve athletes transferring kinetic energy to sports objects. Rolled bowling balls and hit racquetballs have kinetic energy. Some athletes have kinetic energy in their bodies, such as runners racing along a track.

A wrecking ball has potential energy.

building. The potential energy of the wrecking ball now becomes kinetic energy.

## Getting and Storing Energy

Scientists and engineers have experimented with ways of getting and storing energy. Many of these ways of storing energy are very useful.

Solar cells can provide energy to a home.

Magnets use the natural force of magnetism. They are used in everything from computer discs to motors. Electrical lines carry electricity away from power stations where it is made. These lines bring electricity to your home. Batteries make and store chemical energy. Nuclear energy is produced in reactors. Atoms are split apart inside the reactors. This releases energy that is used for electricity. The energy is then stored in another part of the nuclear power plant until it is needed. Much of the power for homes and businesses in the United States is supplied by nuclear energy.

## Clean Energy

Scientists have also found a way to capture energy from the sun. This is called solar power. Horace Bénédict de Saussure built the first solar power collector in 1767. Solar panels capture energy from the sun. This energy is stored in the panels' cells. Solar panels can be mounted on roofs of houses.

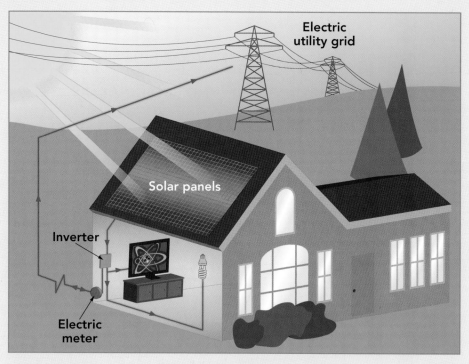

**Harnessing Energy from the Sun**
This diagram shows how solar panels take power from the sun and store it for use as energy in homes. Excess energy can flow back into the utility grid from the house. After reading about solar panels in this chapter, how did you think they sent power to a home? How has that idea changed after looking at this diagram? How does seeing this diagram help you better understand how solar power works?

Another source of clean energy is the wind. Wind is air in motion. Engineers have designed machines that use blades to capture the wind's kinetic energy. The blades are connected to motors that create electricity. In 2011 wind turbines produced 3 percent of the electricity generated in the United States.

# EXPLORE ONLINE

The focus in Chapter Five was on motion and energy. The chapter also touched upon solar energy and other clean energy sources. The Web site below focuses on solar power. As you know, every source is different. How is the information given in the Web site different from the information in this chapter? What information is the same? How do the two sources present information differently? What can you learn from this Web site?

## Energy: Solar Power

video.nationalgeographic.com/video/environment/energy-environment/solar-power

Moving water can also provide usable energy. Scientists and engineers have developed machines to collect the energy in rivers, streams, and oceans. One of these machines is called a wave energy converter. It collects water, which is then run through an engine that stores the energy.

Try to imagine your life in a world and universe not ruled by the laws of forces and motion. Could such a place exist? Could you exist? Forces and motion rule how we move and work every day.

# IMPORTANT DATES

**300s BCE**
Aristotle notices four elements make up the world and believes they cause motion.

**250 BCE**
Archimedes discovers why some objects float or sink.

**1600s CE**
Galileo Galilei experiments with gravity using balls.

**1687**
Sir Isaac Newton writes about the laws of motion.

**1767**
Physicist Horace Bénédict de Saussure builds the first solar power collector.

**1807**
Thomas Young studies how objects in motion can be made to do work.

**1907**
Albert Einstein releases studies on the laws of gravity.

**1990**
On April 24 the Hubble space telescope is launched into space.

**1998**
Stephen Hawking's book *A Brief History of Time* is released on September 1.

**2002**
Gravity Recovery and Climate Experiment (GRACE) satellites are launched on March 17.

**2011**
A Hubble space telescope image shows a fifth moon orbiting Pluto.

# OTHER WAYS YOU CAN FIND FORCES AND MOTION IN THE REAL WORLD

## Beetles with Backpacks

Scientists at the University of Michigan have found a way to get energy from the movement of beetles. This kinetic energy then powers tiny cameras and sensors in a pack strapped to the backs of the insects. The beetles, called "cyborgs," can be sent into dangerous places such as buildings where there has been a chemical spill. The equipment in the beetles' backpacks record information that will let firefighters and other rescuers know if it is safe for them to enter.

## Solar-Powered House Paint

Imagine being able to have solar power in a home by just applying a coat of fresh paint. Researchers at the University of Notre Dame have developed paint that they named "Sun-Believable." It has tiny particles that are able to capture solar power to make energy. Scientists are hoping to make the paint better over time so that it will capture even more solar power.

## Amazing Hovercraft

Hovercrafts are truly all-terrain vehicles. They can travel over land or water. They come in all shapes and sizes, but they have the same three basic parts: a flat surface or platform, a motorized fan, and a skirt. The skirt is on the bottom of the hovercraft and allows it to get over things. Hovercrafts move because the air flowing through chambers in the skirt creates air pressure that is higher than the air pressure outside. This creates an air cushion on which hovercraft ride. They skim approximately 9 inches (23 cm) above surfaces, reducing the friction and making a smooth ride.

### Say What?

Studying forces and motion can mean learning a lot of new vocabulary. Find five words in this book that you've never heard before. Use a dictionary to find out what they mean. Then write the meanings in your own words, and use each word in a new sentence.

### Dig Deeper

What questions do you still have about Newton's laws of motion? Do you want to learn more about how they cause moving objects to behave? Or do you want to study more examples of these laws in action? Write down one or two questions that can guide you in doing your research. With an adult's help, find a few reliable new sources about Newton's laws of motion that can help answer your questions. Write a few sentences about how you did your research and what you learned from it.

## Why Do I Care?

This book explains how forces and motion affect your life every day. List two or three ways that you use forces and motion in your life. For example, what forces do you feel when you ride a bike?

## Tell the Tale

This book discusses the laws of forces and motion, which lead to energy. These laws were not recently discovered. In about 200 words, write the story of the history leading to our understanding of forces and motion. Be sure to set the scene, include several different events, and have a conclusion.

# GLOSSARY

**acceleration**
any increase in speed or change in direction caused by unbalanced forces

**electromagnetic**
the force that holds atoms together

**energy**
the ability to produce work

**forces**
pushes or pulls that can make objects move or stop moving and can change the shape of an object

**friction**
a force that resists or starts the motion of an object

**gravity**
a force that attracts all objects to all other objects

**inertia**
state of objects at rest or in motion in the same direction and at the same speed

**mass**
a measure of the tendency of an object to resist a change in motion

**motion**
any change in position; movement

**theory**
a view of the behavior of our physical world which is testable by experiment and observation

**velocity**
the speed of an object moving in one direction

# LEARN MORE

## Books

Hopwood, James. *Cool Gravity Activities.*
Minneapolis: ABDO, 2008.

Hunter, Rebecca. *The Facts about Forces and Motion.* Mankato, MN: Smart Apple Media, 2004.

Zappa, Marsha. *Black Holes.* Minneapolis: ABDO, 2011.

## Web Links

To learn more about forces and motion, visit ABDO Publishing Company online at **www.abdopublishing.com**. Web sites about forces and motion are featured on our Book Links page. These links are routinely monitored and updated to provide the most current information available. Visit **www.mycorelibrary.com** for free additional tools for teachers and students.

# INDEX

# ABOUT THE AUTHOR

Kathleen M. Muldoon is a retired journalist and columnist. Currently, she is a writing instructor for the Institute of Children's Literature. She has authored 17 books for educational publishers as well as numerous stories and articles for journals and magazines.